# 1999-2000 SPECIAL EDITION

SMASH
# POP
HITS

Project Manager: Carol Cuellar
Cover Design: Martha L. Ramirez

# CONTENTS

# BACK AT ONE

Words and Music by
BRIAN McKNIGHT

6

feel like a lit-tle child whose life has just be-gun. You

came and breathed new life in-to this lone ly heart of mine. You

threw out the life - line, just in the nick of time.

*Chorus:*

One, you're like a dream come true. Two, just wan-na be with you.

# ALL STAR

Tune guitar down a half step

Words and Music by
GREG CAMP

All Star - 7 - 1

12

Verse 3:
It's a cool place and they say it gets colder.
You're bundled up now, wait till you get older.
But the meteor men beg to differ,
Judging by the hole in the satellite picture.
The ice we skate is getting pretty thin.
The water's getting warm, so you might as well swim.
My world's on fire, how about yours?
That's the way I like it and I'll never get bored.
(To Chorus:)

Verse 4:
Somebody once asked, could I spare some change for gas.
I need to get myself away from this place.
I said, "Yep, what a concept;
I could use a little fuel myself
And we could all use a little change."
(To Verse 5:)

# LOVING YOU IS ALL I KNOW

Words and Music by
DIANE WARREN

Loving You Is All I Know - 4 - 1

18

know.

Verse 2:
I can't tell you why stars come out in the evening,
And I can't tell you where they go when they're gone.
And I don't have a clue what makes a flower grow.
Loving you is all I know.
(To Chorus:)

Verse 3:
I can't really say if there is a heaven,
But I feel like it's here when I feel you near me, baby.
I'm not sure of that much, but that's just how it goes.
Loving you is all I know.
(To Chorus:)

*From the Miramax Motion Picture "Music Of The Heart"*

# MUSIC OF MY HEART

Words and Music by
DIANE WARREN

Music of My Heart - 6 - 1

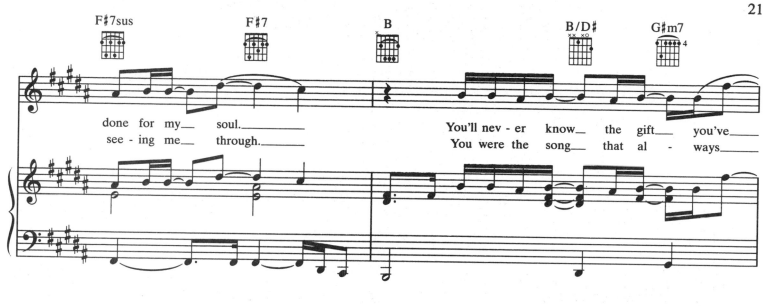

done for my\_ soul._____ You'll nev - er know\_ the gift\_ you've\_

see - ing me\_ through._____ You were the song\_ that al - ways\_

\_ giv - en me._____ I'll car - ry it with me._____

\_ made me sing.\_\_\_\_\_ I'm sing - ing this for you._____

Through the days\_ a - head,\_ I think\_ of days\_ be - fore,\_ when you made me

Ev - 'ry - where\_ I go,\_ I think\_ of where\_ I've been\_ and of the

Music of My Heart - 6 - 2

# AMAZED

Chorus:

I can hear your thoughts, I can see your dreams.

I don't know how you do what you do. I'm so in love with you.

It just keeps get-ting bet-ter.

I wan-na spend the rest of my life with you by my side

for-ev-er and ev-er.

Amazed - 4 - 2

Amazed - 4 - 3

I wan-na spend the rest of my life_____ with you by my side_____ for-ev-er and ev - er.

Ev - 'ry lit - tle thing that you do,_____ (Ev-'ry lit - tle thing that you do . . .)

ev-'ry lit-tle thing that you do, ba-by, I'm a-mazed by_____ you.

**Freely**

*Verse 2:*
The smell of your skin,
The taste of your kiss,
The way you whisper in the dark.
Your hair all around me,
Baby, you surround me;
You touch every place in my heart.
Oh, it feels like the first time every time.
I wanna spend the whole night in your eyes.
*(To Chorus:)*

# ALMOST DOESN'T COUNT

Words and Music by
SHELLY PEIKEN and GUY ROCHE

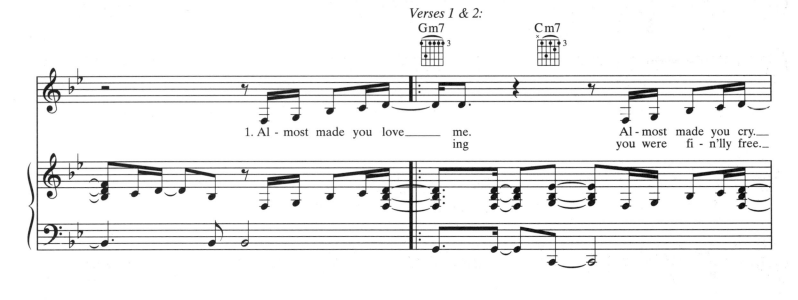

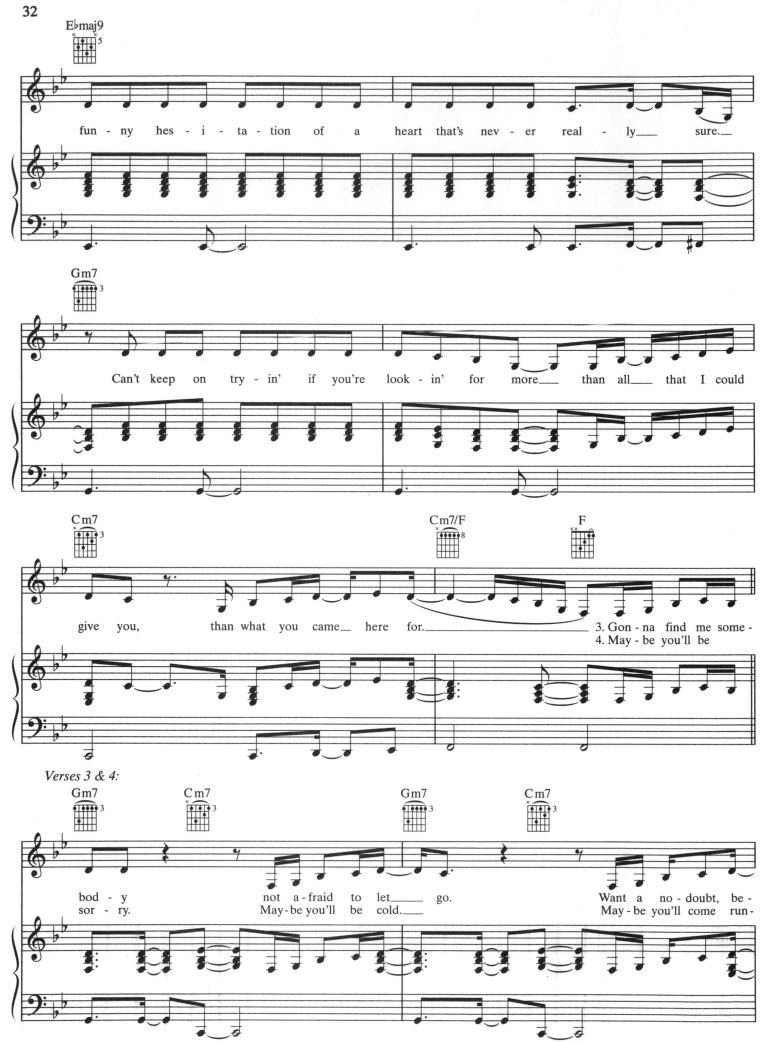

**From the LUCASFILM LTD. Production "STAR WARS: Episode I *The Phantom Menace*"**

# ANAKIN'S THEME

By
JOHN WILLIAMS

Moderato ♩ = 76

*(with pedal)*

Anakin's Theme - 3 - 1

# WHAT A GIRL WANTS

Words and Music by
GUY ROCHE and
SHELLY PEIKEN

Slow, funky groove ♩ = 72

Chorus:

N.C.

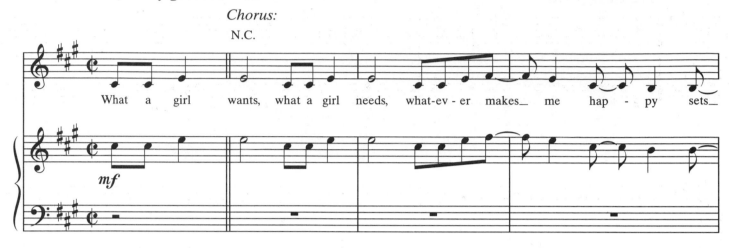

What a girl wants, what a girl needs, what-ev-er makes_ me hap - py sets_

_ you free. What a girl wants, what a girl needs, what-ev-er keeps_ me in_ your arms._

F#m7    A9    Dmaj9    G7

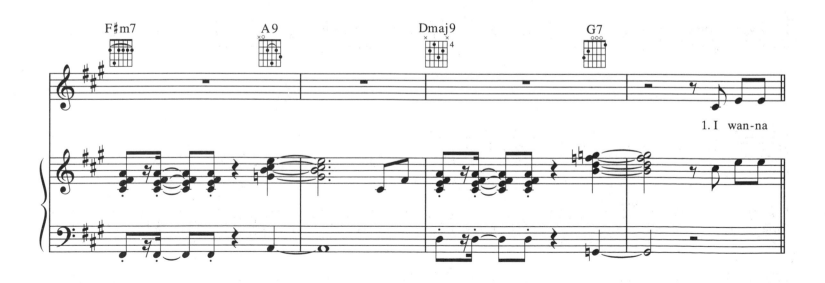

1. I wan-na

44

*Chorus:*

*Verse 2:*
A weaker man might have walked away, but you had faith,
Strong enough to move over and give me space
While I got it together,
While I figured it out.
They say if you love something, let it go;
If it comes back, it's yours.
That's how you know it's for keeps, yeah, it's for sure,
And you're ready and willin' to give me more than...
*(To Chorus:)*

**From the Fox 2000 Motion Picture "ANYWHERE BUT HERE"**

# ANYWHERE BUT HERE

Words and Music by
k.d. lang and RICK NOWELS

*Bridge:*

do do do do do do do. Do do do do do do do, do do do do do do do.

*Coda*

I'll      find      it

*Repeat ad lib. and fade*

an - y - where___      but      here.___

# AS LONG AS YOU LOVE ME

By
MAX MARTIN

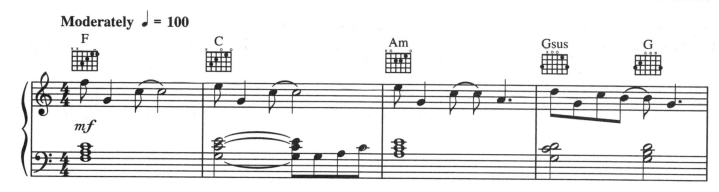

1. Al-though

**Verse 1:**

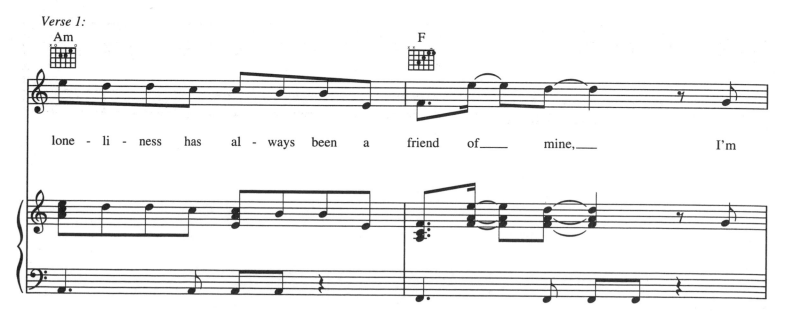

lone - li - ness has al - ways been a friend of_____ mine,_____ I'm

As Long As You Love Me - 7 - 1

# ...BABY ONE MORE TIME

Words and Music by
MAX MARTIN

*From the Motion Picture AUSTIN POWERS: The Spy Who Shagged Me*

# BEAUTIFUL STRANGER

Words and Music by
MADONNA CICCONE and WILLIAM ORBIT

64

66

D.S. % al Coda

C#7

2.

C#7

_____ knows._____

Coda

C#7

C#7sus

_____ knows._____

I paid for you with____

C#7

C#7sus

C#7

_____ tears

and swal-lowed all my____ pride.

E

B

F#

A

C#7sus

Da da da da da da da da da da da da da da._____ Beau - ti - ful

# BAILAMOS

Words and Music by
PAUL BARRY and MARK TAYLOR

*Chorus:*

*Chorus:*

mos,       let the rhy - thm take\_\_ you o - ver, bai - la - mos.\_\_

\_\_       Te quie - ro,      a - mor mi - o,    bai - la -

mos.       Wan - na live this night\_\_ for - ev - er, bai - la - mos.\_\_

*Repeat ad lib. and fade*

\_\_       Te quie - ro,      a - mor mi - o,    bai - la -

# BELIEVE

Words and Music by
BRIAN HIGGINS, STUART McLENNAN,
PAUL BARRY, STEPHEN TORCH,
MATT GRAY and TIM POWELL

* Original recording in G♭ major.

*Chorus:*

*Bridge:*

Believe - 5 - 5

# WAIT TILL I GET HOME

Words and Music by
FULL FORCE

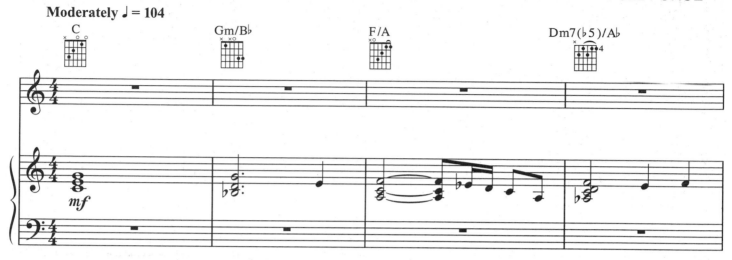

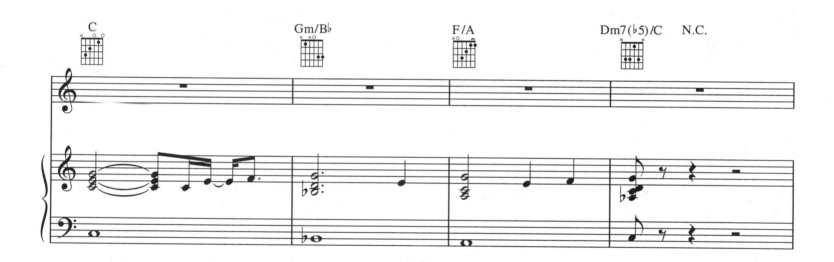

Wait Till I Get Home - 7 - 1

*Chorus:*

*Verse:*

1. Girl, I want to show-er you with my love. Yeah, ba - by, just
2. *See additional lyrics*

wait till I__ get home. Once I get__ you in__ my arms,__ you'll nev - er get e - nough.__

Gm7/C

I need your hug - gin'

Cmaj9       Gm7/C       Cmaj9

and your__ kiss - in'.__ Ba - by, you are the one_____ I've been miss-in'.

*Verse 2:*
Anything you want, baby, I will do for you.
Just wait till I get home.
When it's time for makin' love, we'll rock the whole night through.
Baby, I need your love and affection,
Get things movin' in the right direction.
Six o'clock, time to make love.
Nine o'clock, take a little breather.
Damn, I can't wait to see her when I get home.
*(To Chorus:)*

# C'EST LA VIE

Words and Music by
B*WITCHED, HEDGES BRANNIGAN
and ACKERMAN

Moderately ♩ = 104

*Verse:*

C'est La Vie - 5 - 1

C'est La Vie - 5 - 4

# (YOU DRIVE ME) CRAZY

Words and Music by JÖRGEN ELOFSSON,
DAVID KREUGER, PER MAGNUSSON and MAX MARTIN

Moderately slow ♩ = 92

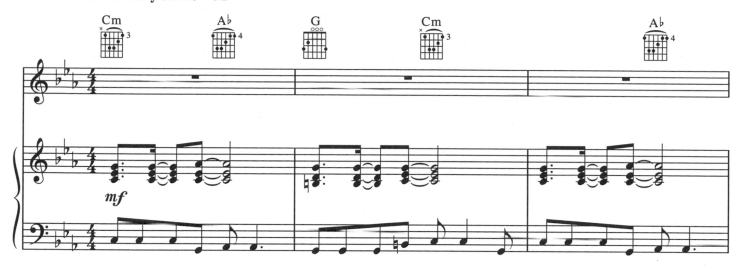

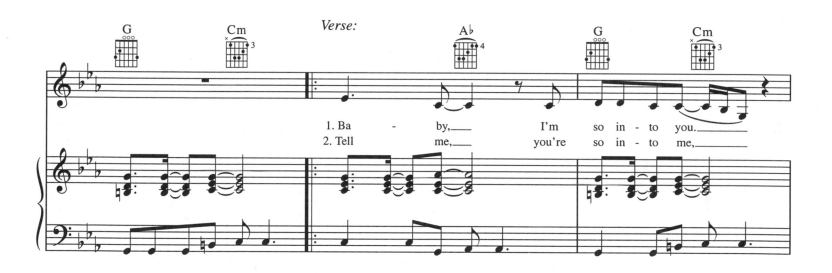

Verse:

1. Ba - by,___ I'm so in - to you.___
2. Tell me,___ you're so in - to me,___

You've got that some - thing. What can I do?___ Ba - by,___ you
that I'm the on - ly one you will see.___ Tell me___ I'm

*Bridge:*

# THE CUP OF LIFE
## (LA COPA DE LA VIDA)

Words and Music by
ROBI ROSA, LUIS G. ESCOLAR
and DESMOND CHILD

Verso:
Cm

1. La vi - da es pu - ra pa - si-ón.___ Hay que lle - nar co -
2. *A letra adicional*

*mf*

pa de a - mor.___ Pa - ra vi - vir hay___ que lu - char.___

Un cor - a - zón pa - ra ga - nar. Co - mo Ca - in y A-bel es un par -

Cm Fm Cm

ti - do_ cruél.___ Tien - es que_ pe - lear_ por un-a es - tre - lla. Con - si - gue

Go!     Go!     Gol!       A - lé,   a - lé,   a - lé._____

*Percussion*

G7               Cm          G7              Cm

G7               Cm

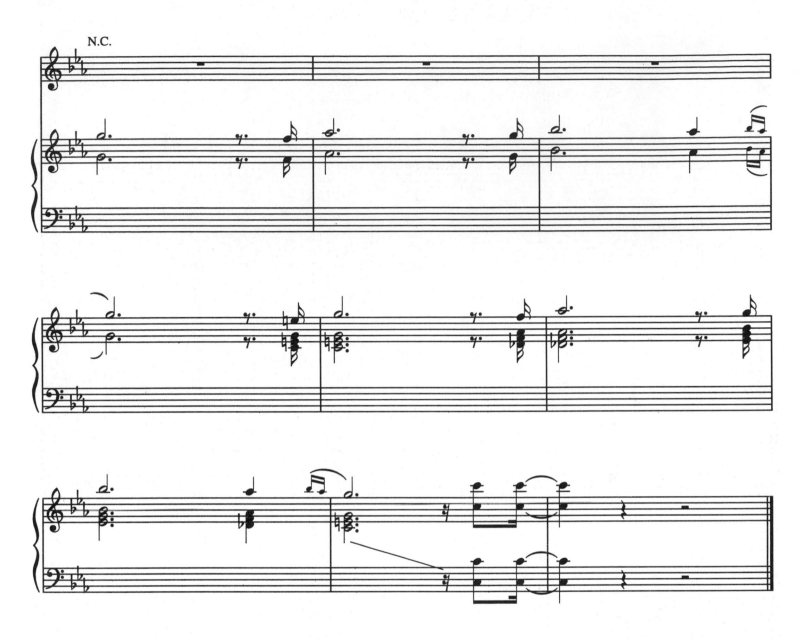

*Verso 2:*
La vida es competición.
Hay que soñar ser campéon.
La copa es la bendicion.
La canaras, go, go, go.
Tu instinto natural.
Vencer a tu rival.
Tienes que pelear por una estrella.
La copa del amor.
Para sobrevivir y luchar por ella.
Luchar por ella. *(Si!)*
Luchar por ella. *(Si!)*
*(Al Coro:)*

# YOU'VE GOT A WAY

Words and Music by
SHANIA TWAIN and R.J. LANGE

Verse 3:
You've got a way with words.
You get me smiling even when it hurts.
There's no way to measure what your love is worth.
I can't believe the way you get through to me.
(To Chorus:)

# THAT'S THE WAY IT IS

Words and Music by
MAX MARTIN, KRISTIAN LUNDIN
and ANDREAS CARLSSON

112 *Chorus:*

*Music From and Inspired By the Motion Picture POKÉMON - THE FIRST MOVIE*

# DON'T SAY YOU LOVE ME

Words and Music by
MARION RAVN, MARIT LARSEN,
PETER ZIZZO and JIMMY BRALOWER

Don't Say You Love Me - 6 - 1

*Verses 2 & 3:*

2. You're mov - ing too fast, I don't un - der - stand you.
3. Here's how I play, here's where you stand.

I'm not read - y yet. Ba - by, I can't pre - tend, no, I can't.
Here's what to prove to get an - y fur - ther than where it's been.

The best I can do is tell you to talk to me. It's pos - si - ble, e -
I'll make it clear; not gon - na tell you twice. Take it slow, you keep

ven - tu - al. Love will find a way. (Love will find a way.)
push - ing me. You're push - ing me a - way. (Push - ing me a - way.)

*Chorus:*

*Chorus:*

# DOWN SO LONG

Words and Music by
JEWEL KILCHER

I take a trip, I catch a train, I catch a plane, I got a tick-et in my__ hand,__ and then a

*D.S.% al Coda*

fat man takes my mon-ey and like cat-tle we all stand.__

*Coda*

end__ must be, oh, I know the end__ must be, oh, I know the

end__ must be draw-ing__ near.__

*Repeat ad lib. and fade*

*Verse 3:*
I look to everybody but me to answer my prayers,
Till I saw an angel in a bathroom who said she saw no one worth saving anywhere.
And a blind man on the corner said it's simple, like flipping a coin:
Don't matter what side it lands on if it's someone else's dime.
*(To Chorus:)*

# WHEN I SAID I DO

Words and Music by
CLINT BLACK

When I Said I Do - 4 - 1

128

When I Said I Do - 4 - 3

**Verse 2:**
Well, this old world keeps changin'
And the world stays the same
For all who came before.
And it goes hand in hand,
Only you and I can undo
All that we became.
That makes us so much more

Than a woman and a man.
And after everything that comes and goes around
Has only passed us by,
Here alone in our dreams,
I know there's a lonely heart in every lost and found.
But forever you and I will be the ones
Who found out what forever means.
*(To Chorus:)*

# FROM THIS MOMENT ON

Words and Music by
SHANIA TWAIN and R.J. LANGE

From This Moment On - 7 - 1

for better, for worse, I will love you with ev - 'ry beat___ of my heart.___

1. From this

**Slowly** ♩ = 72
*Verse 1:*

mo - ment life has be - gun.___ From this mo - ment___

you are the one.___ Right be - side___ you is where I be - long,

132

Verse 2:

from this mo - ment on._____ 2. From this mo - ment I have been blessed._

_ I live on - ly for your hap - pi - ness.__ And for your_

_ love I'd give my last breath,_____ from this mo - ment on._

Chorus:

_ I give my hand_ to you__ with all_ my heart._____ Can't

134

# GENIE IN A BOTTLE

Words and Music by
PAMELA SHEYNE, DAVID FRANK
and STEVE KIPNER

Genie in a Bottle - 5 - 1

138

*Chorus:*

If you want to be with me, ba-by, there's a price to pay. I'm a ge-nie in a bot-

tle, you got-ta rub me the right way. If you want to be with

me, I can make your wish come true. { You got-ta make a big___ im-pres-  
{ Just come and set me

sion, I got-ta like what you do._____  
free, and, ba-by, I'll be with you.___ I'm a ge-nie in a bot-tle, ba-by,

*To Coda*

# GOODBYE

Words and Music by
RICHARD STANNARD, MATT ROWE, MELANIE BROWN,
VICTORIA AADAMS, EMMA BUNTON and MELANIE CHISHOLM

Verse 2:
Just a little girl, big imagination
Never letting no-one take it away
Went into the world, what a revelation
She found there's a better way for you and me to be.
Look for the rainbow in ev'ry storm
Find out for certain love's gonna be there for you
You'll always be someone's baby.

Goodbye my friend *etc.*

𝄋:
Look for the rainbow in ev'ry storm
Find out for certain love's gonna be there for you
You'll always be someone's baby.

# HEARTBREAKER

Words and Music by
MARIAH CAREY, NARADA MICHAEL WALDEN,
JEFFREY COHEN, SHIRLEY ELLISTON and LINCOLN CHASE

Moderately slow ♩ = 92

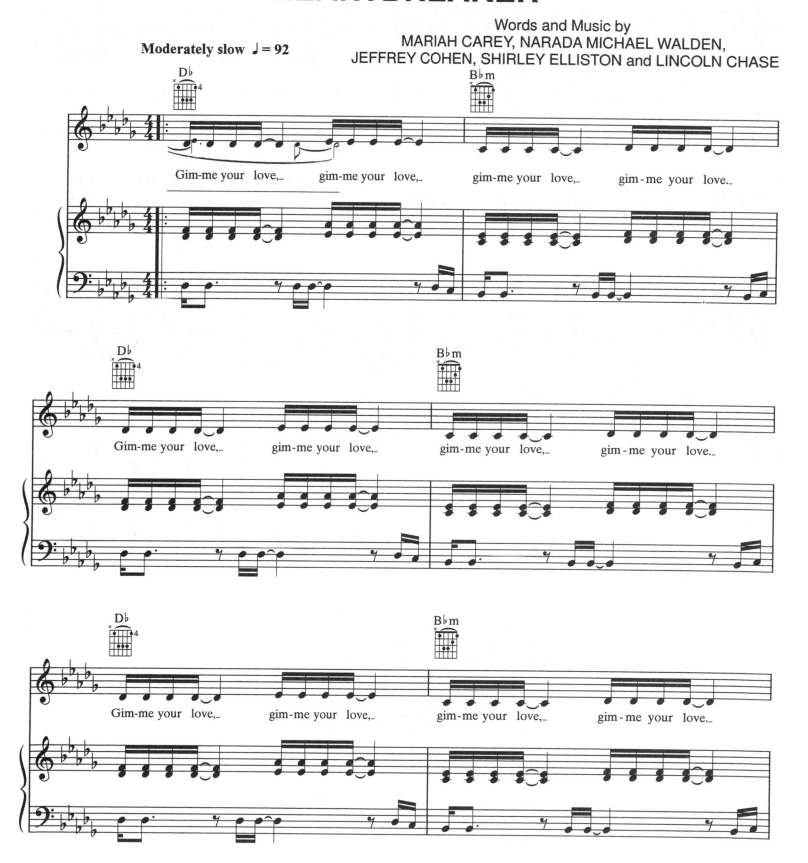

Heartbreaker - 7 - 1

148

Heartbreaker - 7 - 2

Chorus:

Gim-me your love,_ gim-me your love,_ gim-me your love,_ gim-me your love._

*Verse 2:*
It's a shame to be so euphoric and weak
When you smile at me and you tell me the things that you know
Persuade me to relinquish my love to you,
But I cannot resist at all.
*(To Pre-chorus:)*

*Rap:*
*She wanna shop with Jay, play box with Jay,*
*She wanna pillow fight in the middle of the night.*
*She wanna drive my Benz with five of my friends,*
*She wanna creep past the block, spyin' again.*
*She wanna roll with Jay, chase ski hoes away.*
*She wanna fight with lame chicks, blow my day.*
*She wanna inspect the rest, kick me to the curb*
*If she find one strand of hair longer than hers.*
*She want love in the Jacuzzi, rub up in the movies.*
*Access to the old crib, keys to the newbies.*
*She wanna answer the phone, tattoo her arm.*
*That's when I gotta send her back to her mom.*
*She called me heartbreaker.*
*When we're apart it makes her*
*Want a piece of paper, scribble down, "I hate ya."*
*But she know she love Jay because*
*She love everything Jay say, Jay does.*
*(To Chorus:)*

# I COULD NOT ASK FOR MORE

Words and Music by
DIANE WARREN

# I DO (CHERISH YOU)

Words and Music by
KEITH STEGALL and DAN HILL

*Enharmonic chord labeling of F♭maj7.

Verse 2:
In my world before you,
I lived outside my emotions.
Didn't know where I was going
Till that day I found you.
How you opened my life
To a new paradise.
In a world torn by change,
Still with all of my heart,
Till my dying day . . .
(To Chorus:)

*From Touchstone Pictures' ARMAGEDDON*

# I DON'T WANT TO MISS A THING

Words and Music by
DIANE WARREN

I Don't Want to Miss a Thing - 7 - 1

*Chorus:*

*Repeat ad lib. and fade*

# I LOVE YOU CAME TOO LATE

Words and Music by
ERIC FOSTER WHITE and MIKEY BASSIE

I Love You Came Too Late - 4 - 1

Dm/F   F   1. Em/G   G   2. Em/G   G

I love___ you came___ too late.___ you came___ too late.
I can't

Am   E+/G#   C/G

live with-out you. Don't want no-bod-y else.___ My heart is in___ my hand.___ I took a

D9   Em7

good look at___ my-self._____ If I had an-oth-er chance,___ I'd

A7   Dm7   Fm6

shout it out to___ the world._____ I love___ you.

*Chorus:*

*Repeat ad lib. and fade*

Verse 2:
I should have seen the signs,
Paid her more attention.
But I pushed her love away,
So she found someone
To give her what she needed,
Somebody else not afraid to say . . .
I can't live without you,
Don't want nobody else.
Baby, listen very closely,
I love you.
(To Chorus:)

# I STILL BELIEVE

Words and Music by
ANTONINA ARMATO
and BEPPE CANTORELLI

*Chorus:*

I still be - lieve,___ some - day you and me_____ will

find our - selves in love___ a - gain._____

I had a dream,___ some - day you and me_____ will

*Repeat ad lib. and fade*

find our - selves in love___ a - gain._____

# I WANT IT THAT WAY

Words and Music by
MAX MARTIN and
ANDREAS CARLSSON

182

*Bridge:*

that way.___ Now I can see___ that we've fall - en a - part___ from the

way that it used___ to___ be,___ yeah.___ No mat - ter the dis - tance, I

want you to know___ that deep down in - side___ of me___ you are___

___ my fi - re,___ the one___ de -

I Want It That Way - 5 - 3

184

*Chorus:*

# I WILL BE RIGHT HERE

Words and Music by
DIANE WARREN

*Chorus:*

what - ev - er you do,_____ wher - ev - er you are,_____ my heart_ is with_

_ you. No mat-ter how far,_____ I'll al - ways be near._____ When-ev - er you need_ me,

I will be right here.

_ me, I will be right here. And when the

188

*From The Fox Searchlight Film, "THE BROTHERS McMULLEN"*

# I WILL REMEMBER YOU

Words and Music by
SARAH McLACHLAN, SEAMUS EGAN
and DAVE MERENDA

I Will Remember You - 4 - 1

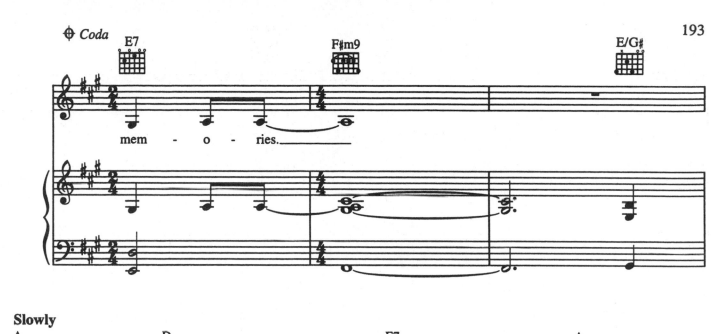

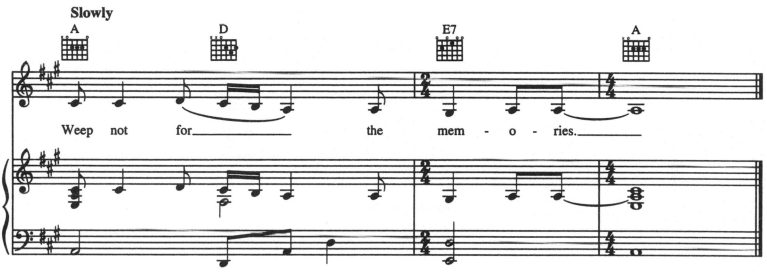

*Verse 2:*
So afraid to love you,
More afraid to lose.
I'm clinging to a past
That doesn't let me choose.
Where once there was a darkness,
A deep and endless night,
You gave me everything you had,
Oh, you gave me life.
*(To Chorus:)*

*(Optional Verse 1 — Album version)*
Remember the good times that we had,
I let them slip away from us when things got bad.
Now clearly I first saw you smiling in the sun.
I wanna feel your warmth upon me,
I wanna be the one.
*(To Chorus:)*

# I'LL STILL LOVE YOU MORE

Words and Music by
DIANE WARREN

I'll Still Love You More - 4 - 2

I'll still love you more._

And for ev-'ry kiss, I'll kiss you back_ a hun-dred times. And for ev-'ry-thing you do, I'll just do

more._____ And for all the love you give, I'll give you so__ much back, you'll see.____ Got

so much love for you__ in-side me. If you

*Bridge:*

*Verse 2:*
Ask me just what I'd do for you;
I'll tell you that I would do anything.
Ask if this heart beats true for you;
I'll show you a truer heart could never be.
You could say there's not a star that you won't bring me.
You could say there'll be no day that you won't need me.
You could think no other love could last as long,
But you'd be wrong,
You'd be wrong.
*(To Chorus:)*

# I'LL NEVER BREAK YOUR HEART

By
ALBERT MANNO and
EUGENE WILDE

Slowly ♩. = 66

Spoken: Baby, I know you are hurting; right now you feel like you could never love again. Now all I ask is for a chance

Verse:

to prove that I love you.  1.From the first day that I saw___ your smil-ing face,___ hon-ey, I
2. See additional lyrics

knew___ that we would be to-geth-er for-ev-er.  Ooh, when I

I'll Never Break Your Heart - 5 - 1

200

I'll Never Break Your Heart - 5 - 3

*Verse 2:*
As I walked by you,
Will you get to know me
A little more better?
Girl, that's the way love goes.
And I know you're afraid
To let your feelings show,
And I understand.
But girl, it's time to let go.

I deserve a try, honey,
Just once,
Give me a chance
And I'll prove this all wrong.
You walked in,
You were so quick to judge,
But honey, he's nothing like me.
Darling, why can't you see?
*(To Chorus:)*

# I'VE DREAMED OF YOU

Words and Music by
ANN HAMPTON CALLAWAY
and ROLF LOVLAND

dreamed of you,                al - ways feel - ing you                were there.
just when I_____ thought love had passed me by,            we met.

I've Dreamed of You - 5 - 1

# IF I COULD TURN BACK THE HANDS OF TIME

Words and Music by
R. KELLY

If I Could Turn Back the Hands of Time - 6 - 1

*Vamp:*

2. There'd be nothing I wouldn't do for you,
   Forever honest and true to you.
   If you accept me back in your heart, I love you.
3. Woah, that would be my will.
   Darlin', I'm begging you to take me by the hands.
4. I'm goin' down, yes, I am.
   Down on my bended knee, yeah.
   And I'm gonna be right there until you return to me.
5. Woah, if I could just turn back that little clock on the wall,
   Then I'd come to realize how much I love you.

# JUPITER

Words and Music by
JEWEL KILCHER

Tune guitar: D-A-D-G-B-E

*Chorus:*

stars from my crown, let the years fall down.__ Lay me

out in fi - re - light,__ let my skin feel the night. Fas - ten

me to your side,__ (2.) and say it will be soon._____ You

make me so__ cra - zy, ba - by, could swal - low the

218

# IT'S ALL ABOUT YOU
## (NOT ABOUT ME)

Words and Music by
HEAVYNN LUMPKINS, KENNETH KARLIN
and CARSTEN "SOULSHOCK" SCHACK

Slowly ♩ = 69

1. When we first met, you stole my heart a-way.
2. *See additional lyrics*

Your love was in-cred-i-ble, won-der-ful, then you be-gan to change.

It's All About You - 5 - 1

*Chorus:*

Bridge:

An - y - thing___ you want, I'll do. I'll nev - er un - der - stand how you could

treat me bad___ and be so cruel. You're beg - gin' me___ to come back to you. Had

faith in you___ and gave all my love, but what I had___ was not e - nough. You

*Chorus:*

B♭m7

E♭m9

B♭m7

E♭m9

*Repeat ad lib. and fade*

turned a-round___ and broke my trust. Got the nerve to ask___ me what a-bout us.

I, I tried to be___ the one for, ba-by, you, you. Nev-er was___ e-nough in what I

do, do. That's why___ I'm leav-ing, 'cause it's all a-bout___ you and not a-bout me.___

*Verse 2:*
When we get in a fight,
I'm always the first to apologize.
Even if it was you who did wrong.
I'd never do enough to please you,
That's why I can't go on.
No matter what I do for you,
It's never any good for you.
You always gotta complain,
That's why I gotta say,
I can't stay.
*(To Chorus:)*

# (God Must Have Spent)
# A LITTLE MORE TIME ON YOU

Words and Music by
CARL STURKEN and EVAN ROGERS

Can this be true?__ Tell me,
all of cre - a - tion, all things

can this be real?_____
great and small, ___

How can I put_____ in - to words _
you are the one_____ that sur - pass -

A liitle More Time On You - 5 - 1

# LARGER THAN LIFE

Words and Music by
MAX MARTIN, KRISTIAN LUNDIN
and BRIAN T. LITTRELL

Rock ♩ = 120

N.C.

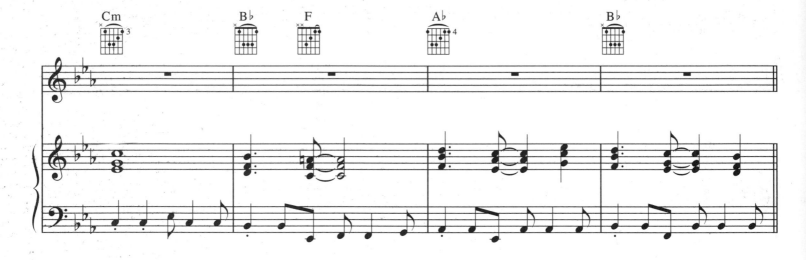

Larger Than Life - 6 - 1

*Chorus:*

keeps us___ a - live.___

*cresc.*

(Inst. solo ad lib. . . .)

*mf*

. . . end solo)

*Chorus:*

All you peo - ple, can't you see, can't you see how___ your love's af - fect - ing our re -

*Chorus:*

All you peo-ple, can't you see, can't you see how____ your love's af-fect-ing our re-al-i-ty?____ Ev- 'ry time we're down, you____ can make it right and that makes____ you larg -er,____ that makes____ you larg -er,____ that makes____ you larg -er____ than____ life.

# LET ME LET GO

Words and Music by
DENNIS MORGAN and
STEVE DIAMOND

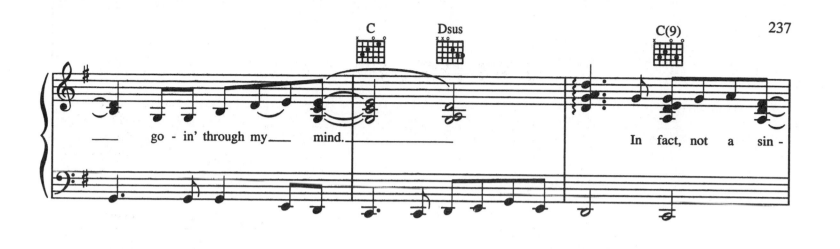

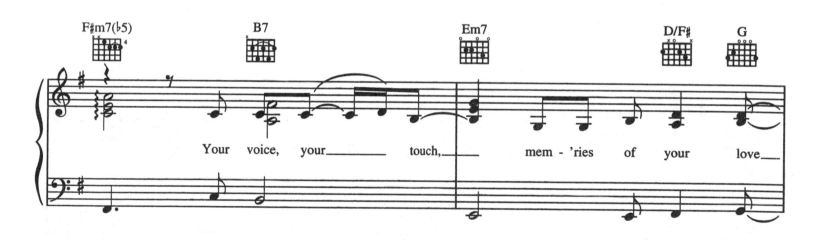

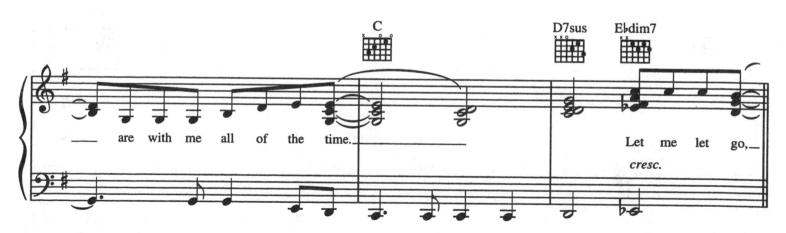

why are you still in my heart,___ are you still in my

soul?___ Let me let go.___

**Bridge:**

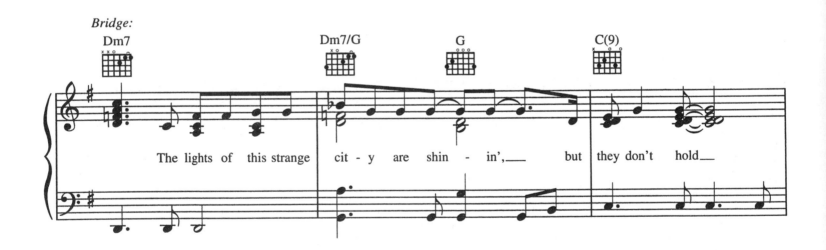

The lights of this strange cit - y are shin - in',___ but they don't hold___

no fas - ci - na - tion for me.___ I try to find___ the bright side, ba - by, but

# LIVIN' LA VIDA LOCA

Words and Music by
ROBI ROSE and DESMOND CHILD

Verse 1:

1. She's in-to su-per-sti-tions, black cats and voo-doo dolls.

I feel a pre-mo-ni-tion, that girl's gon-na make me fall.___

**Verses 2 & 3:**

2. She's in-to new sen-sa-tions, new kicks in the can-dle-light.___
3. *See additional lyrics*

She's got a new ad-dic-tion for ev-'ry day and night.___ 1. She'll

248

*Verse 3:*
Woke up in New York City
In a funky, cheap hotel.
She took my heart and she took my money.
She must have slipped me a sleeping pill.

*Bridge 2:*
She never drinks the water
And makes you order French champagne.
Once you've had a taste of her
You'll never be the same.
Yeah, she'll make you go insane.
*(To Chorus:)*

# ROLLERCOASTER

Words and Music by
B*WITCHED, HEDGES, BRANNIGAN
and ACKERMAN

Rollercoaster - 5 - 1

*Verse:*

days' the day,___ we're out to play___ and lost our way.___ It's
don't be shy,___ you'll soon be high.___ We'll touch the sky,___ you'll

al - ways the same,___ oh, baby, now.___ Climbed the trees,___ swam the
nev - er be - lieve,___ oh, ba - by, now. Go 'round and 'round,___ but

sev - en seas,___ we've grazed our knees___ and no one's to blame,. oh.___
don't look down.. We won't be found,. you'd bet - ter be - lieve___ it.___

*Pre-chorus:*

1.2. Come and sit be - side us, we'll give you such a thrill. We're not nice, we're cool as ice, we'll

252

# LOST IN YOU

Words and Music by
TOMMY SIMS, GORDON KENNEDY
and WAYNE KIRKPATRICK

Lost in You - 4 - 1

# LOVE LIKE OURS

Lyrics by
ALAN and MARILYN BERGMAN

Music by
DAVE GRUSIN

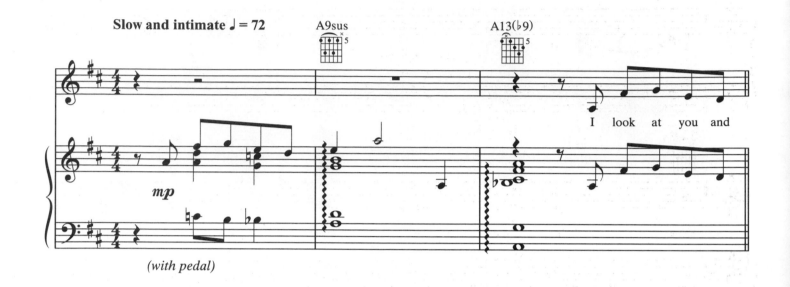

Love Like Ours - 4 - 1

259

Love Like Ours - 4 - 2

**Page 261**

Lyrics: we guard it with our lives. What - ev - er goes a - stray, what rain - y day comes a - round, a love like ours will keep us safe and sound.

Love Like Ours - 4 - 4

# MAN! I FEEL LIKE A WOMAN!

Words and Music by
SHANIA TWAIN and R.J. LANGE

Verse 1:

Man! I Feel Like a Woman! - 6 - 2

Verse 3:
The girls need a break.
Tonight we're gonna take
The chance to get out on the town.
We don't need romance.
We only wanna dance.
We're gonna let our hair hang down.
The best thing about being a woman
Is the prerogative to have a little fun and...
(To Chorus:)

# MY NAME IS

Words and Music by
LABI SIFFRE

Moderately slow ♩ = 92

*Chorus:*

Hi, my name is...What? My name is... Who? My name is Slim Shad - y.

Hi, my name is...What? My name is... Who? My name is Slim Shad - y.

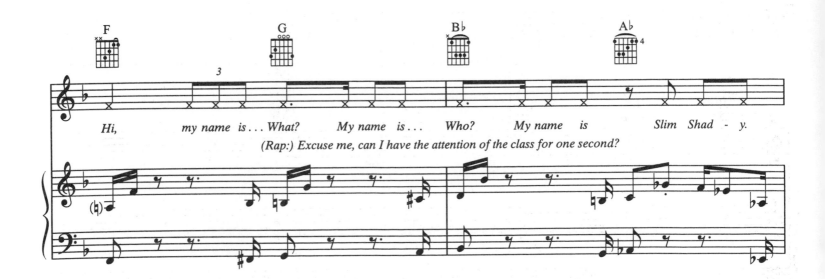

Hi, my name is...What? My name is... Who? My name is Slim Shad - y.
*(Rap:) Excuse me, can I have the attention of the class for one second?*

My Name Is - 4 - 1

*Chorus:*

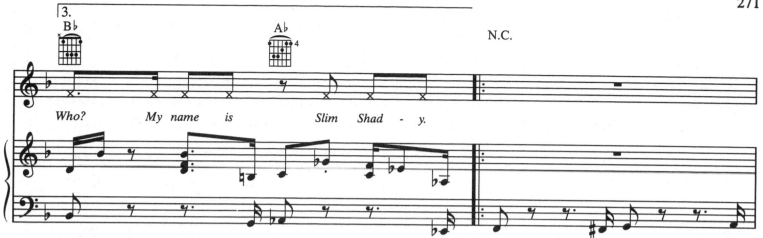

Who?        My  name    is         Slim   Shad  -  y.

Repeat ad lib. and fade

**Verse 1:**
*Hi, kids! Do you like Primus?*
*Wanna see me stick nine-inch nails*
*Through each one of my eyelids?*
*Wanna copy me and do exactly like I did?*
*Try 'cid and get ******-up worse than my life is?*
*My brain's dead weight.*
*I'm trying to get my head straight,*
*But I can't figure out which Spice Girl I wanna impregnate.*
*And Dr. Dre said, "Slim Shady, you're perverted."*
*I know, but, "Just watch your mouth.*
*This is the clean version."*
*Well, since age twelve, I felt like a caged elf*
*Who stayed to himself in one place chasing this tail.*
*Got ticked-off and ripped Pamela Lee's lips off,*
*Kissed 'em and said,*
*"I ain't know silicone was supposed to be this soft."*
*I'm 'bout to pass out and crash and fall in the grass,*
*Faster than a fat man who sat down too fast.*
*Come here, lady!*
*"Shady, wait a minute, that's my girl dog."*
*I don't give a damn,*
*Dre sent me to tick the world off.*
*(To Chorus:)*

**Verse 2:**
*My English teacher wanted to flunk me in junior high.*
*Thanks a lot. Next semester, I'll be thirty-five.*
*I smacked him in his face with an eraser,*
*Chased him with a stapler,*
*And told him to change the grade on the paper.*
*Walked into the strip club, had my jacket zipped up.*
*Flashed the bartender and stuck my **** in her tip cup.*
*Extraterrestrial running over pedestrians in a spaceship*
*While they're screaming at me, "Let's just be friends."*
*Ninety-nine percent of my life, I was lied to.*
*I just found out my mom does more **** than I do.*
*I told her I'd grow up to be a famous rapper,*
*Make a record about doin' ***** and name it after her.*
*You know you blew up when the women rush the stage*
*And try to touch your hands like some screaming Usher fans.*
*This guy at White Castle asked me for my autograph.*
*So I signed it, "Dear Dave, thanks for the support. *******!"*
*(To Chorus:)*

**Verse 3:**
*Stop the tape, this kid needs to be locked away.*
*Get him!*
*Dr. Dre, don't just stand there . . . operate!*
*I'm not ready to leave, it's too scary to die.*
*I'd rather be carried inside the cemetery and buried alive.*
*Am I coming or going? I can barely decide.*
*I just drank a fifth of Coolade; dare me to drive?*
*Go ahead. All of my life I was very deprived.*
*I ain't had a woman in years*
*And my palms are too hairy to hide.*
*Clothes ripped like The Incredible Hulk.*
*I spit when I talk, I **** anything that walks.*
*Come here!*
*When I was little, I used to get so hungry I would throw fits.*
*"How you gonna breast-feed me, Mom, you ain't got no ****?"*
*I lay awake and strap myself in the bed,*
*With a bulletproof vest on and tapped myself in the head,*
*'Cause I'm steamin' mad.*
*And by the way, when you see my dad,*
*Ask him if he bought a porno mag and seen my ad.*
*(To Chorus:)*

My Name Is - 4 - 4

# NO SCRUBS

Words and Music by
KEVIN BRIGGS, KANDI BURRIS
and TAMEKA COTTLE

Moderately ♩ = 100

*Verse:*

scrub is a guy that thinks__ he's fly __ and is al - so known as a bust - er.__
me. 2. *See additional lyrics*

No Scrubs - 6 - 1

Verse 2:
But a scrub is checkin' me,
But his game is kinda weak.
And I know that he can't approach me,
'Cause I'm lookin' like class and he's lookin' like trash.
'Can't get wit' no deadbeat ass. So
No, I don't want your number,
No, I don't want to give you mine,
No, I don't want to meet you nowhere,
No, I don't want none of your time.
And . . .
(To Chorus:)

# NOBODY'S SUPPOSED TO BE HERE

Words and Music by
MONTELL JORDAN and ANTHONY "SHEP" CRAWFORD

Slowly

How did you get here? No-bod-y's s'posed to be here. I've tried that love thing for the last time. My

Nobody's Supposed to Be There - 6 - 1

# NOTHING REALLY MATTERS

Words and Music by
MADONNA CICCONE and
PATRICK LEONARD

Moderately ♩ = 104

Verse:

1. When I was ver - y___ young,___
2. Look - ing at my___ life,___

noth-ing real-ly mat - tered___ to me_____  but mak - ing___ my -
it's ver - y clear to___ me._____  I lived___ so

Nothing Really Matters - 6 - 1

286

Nothing Really Matters - 6 - 3

# THE PRAYER

Italian Lyric by
**ALBERTO TESTA and TONY RENIS**

Words and Music by
**CAROLE BAYER SAGER and DAVID FOSTER**

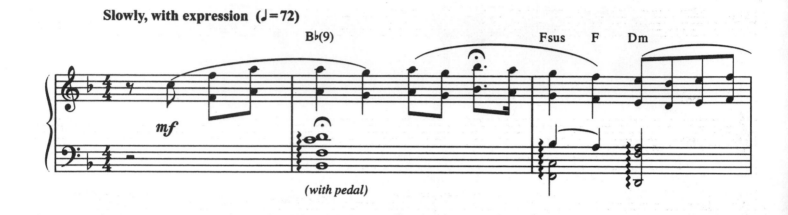

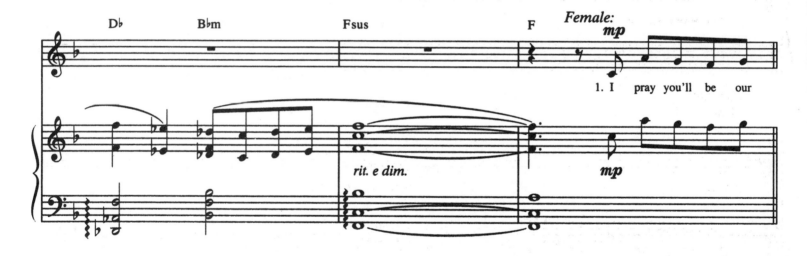

The Prayer - 8 - 1

Chorus:

# SHAKE YOUR BON-BON

Words and Music by
ROBI ROSA, GEORGE NORIEGA
and DESMOND CHILD

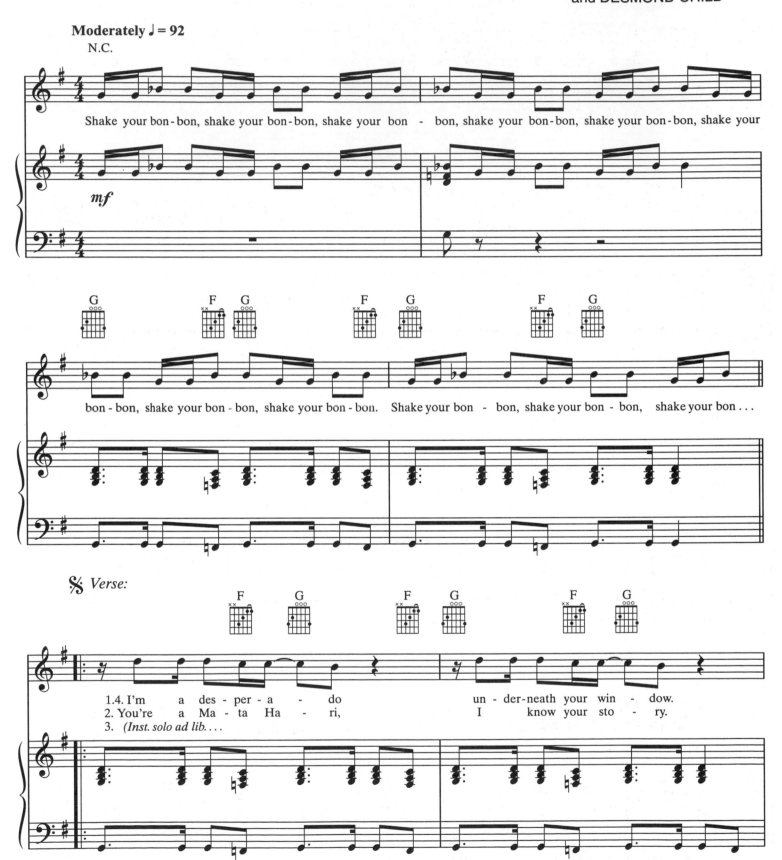

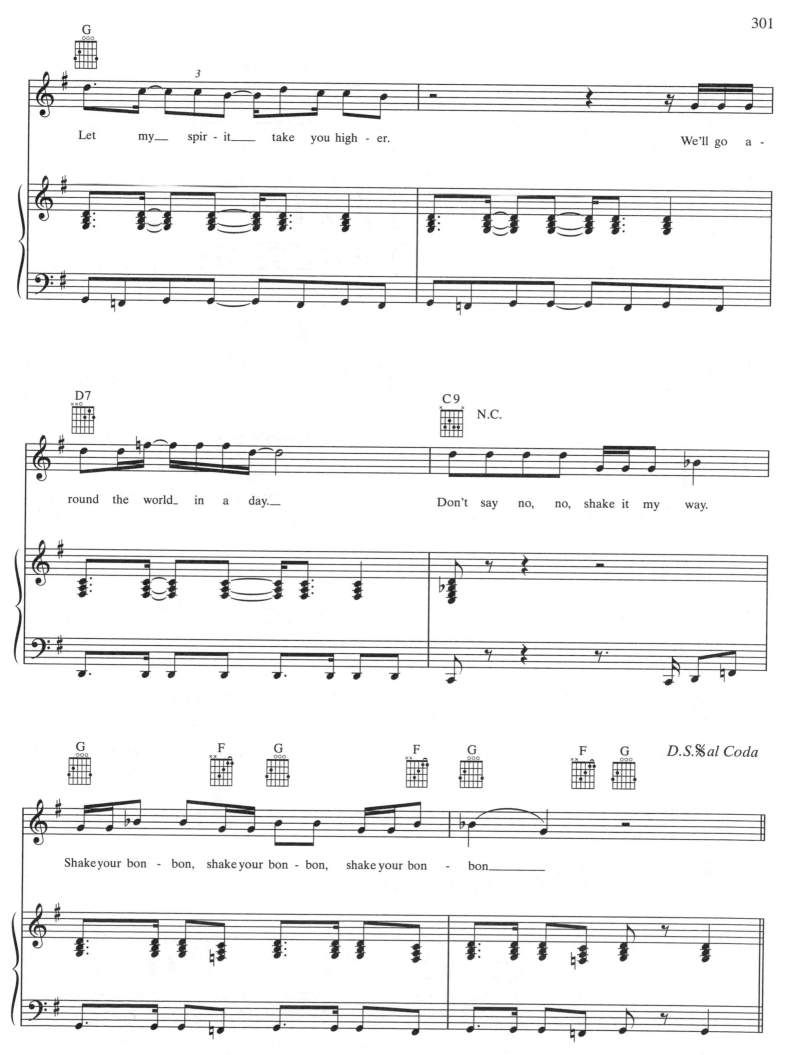

302

'Round the world, we'll do the Fan - dan - go. Shake your bon-bon, shake your bon - bon, shake your bon -

bon, shake your bon - bon, shake your bon - bon, shake your bon - bon. Shake_ your bon - bon,_ ba -

Repeat ad lib. and fade

by.                                    Shake_ your bon - bon,_ ba - by.

# SMILE

Words and Music by
JOSH DEUTSCH and COLLEEN FITZPATRICK

Moderately ♩ = 92

Smile - 5 - 1

Put a smile 'pon your face and greet one and all.___

Verse 2:
*And another thing . . .*
You can say that I'm a dreamer
And you think it's so cool,
Preachin' 'bout the better life I learned in school.
But you get what you give in this life that we live,
And all that you do will come back to you.
Life, (life,) it ain't easy,
It's so tough, (life,) it ain't easy.
Whatcha wanna do, say whatcha gonna do?
*(To Chorus:)*

Bridge:(Rap:)
*Yo, when things isn't right, there's no need to fight.*
*From you have life then everything nice.*
*Love all your elders, please be polite.*
*Even when you're hurting, don't forget to smile.*
*Give love to all nation big or small.*
*When you do good you'll get your reward.*
*United we stand, divided we fall.*
*(Sung:)*
Put a smile on your face and greet one and all.
Life, (life,) it ain't easy,
It's so tough, (life,) it ain't easy.
Whatcha wanna do, say whatcha gonna do?
*(To Chorus:)*

Smile - 5 - 5

# SHE'S ALL I EVER HAD

Words and Music by
ROBI ROSA, GEORGE NORIEGA
and JON SECADA

Moderately slow ♩ = 82

*Verse:*

1. Here I am,___ bro - ken wings.___
2. So much time,___ so much pain, but

Qui - et thoughts,___ un - spo - ken dreams.___
there's one thing___ that still___ re - mains.___

She's All I Ever Had - 6 - 1

311

She's All I Ever Had - 6 - 4

# SMOOTH

Lyrics by
ROB THOMAS

Music by ITAAL SHUR
and ROB THOMAS

Smooth - 5 - 1

Smooth - 5 - 4

318

Verse 2:
Well, I'll tell you one thing,
If you would leave, it be a crying shame.
In every breath and every word
I hear your name calling me out, yeah.
Well, out from the barrio,
You hear my rhythm on your radio.
You feel the tugging of the world,
So soft and slow, turning you 'round and 'round.
(To Pre-Chorus:)

# SOMETIMES

Words and Music by
JÖRGEN ELOFSSON

F/A    F    Cm11                              F7sus

want to stay,                but ev-'ry time you   come too close, I move a - way.⎤
wait for me,                 you'll see   that    you're the on - ly one for me.⎦

Cm11                 F7sus                        B♭        F/A

I wan - na be - lieve___ in ev - 'ry-thing that you say,___          'cause it sounds

Gm                   Cm7                          B♭

so___    good.___    But if you real - ly want___ me,   move___ slow.___   There's

*Chorus:*

Cm11                            F7sus               B♭

things a - bout___ me you just have to know.___   Some-times I run,___          some-times

I hide. Some - times I'm scared___ of you.___ But all I real - ly want is to hold___

___ you tight,___ treat you right, be with you day___ and night.___

Ba - by, all I need is time. All I real - ly want is to hold___ you tight,___ treat

you right, be with you day___ and night.___ Ba - by, all I need is time.

*Bridge:*

# SPECIAL

Words and Music by
DOUG ERIKSON, SHIRLEY MANSON,
STEVE MARKER and BUTCH VIG

Tune guitar down a half step

*Chorus:*

# STRONG ENOUGH

Words and Music by
MARK TAYLOR and
PAUL BARRY

**Moderate dance** ♩ = 132

*Verse 1:*

Strong Enough - 7 - 1

330

And I hear___ your___ rea - sons why.___ Where did___ you sleep___ ___ last night?___ And was___ she worth___ it? Was___ ___ she worth_____ it? 'Cause I'm strong___

Chorus:

___ e - nough to live___ with - out___ you, strong___ e - nough. And I___

*Verse 2:*

# STAY THE SAME

Words and Music by
JOEY McINTYRE and JOE CARRIER

**Slowly** ♩ = 72

**§ Chorus:**

Don't you ev - er wish you were\_ some - one else.\_ You were meant to be\_ the

*Verse:*

change. I think that you could be___ what-ev-er you want-ed to be___ if you could

re - al -ize___ all the dreams you have___ in - side.___

Don't be a-fraid___ if you've got some-thing to say,___ just

o - pen up___ your heart___ and let it show you the way.___

*D.S. 𝄋 al Coda*

# TAKE ME THERE

Words and Music by
TEDDY RILEY, TAMARA SAVAGE, MASON BETHA,
MICHAEL FOSTER, MADELINE NELSON and MARK MOTHERSBAUGH

Take Me There - 6 - 1

*Rap (See additional lyrics)*

(Drums)

1–3

*(Rap continues)*

4

Just take ___ me there. *(first time only)*
Take me there. I wan-na go there.
*Lead vocal ad lib.*

Take me there. Let's go there. Take me to that ___ great place with

Am                  F     Dm7           G

won - ders and wish - es.     Take me there.    I wan-na go there.

C             Am            Bdim        E7

Take me there.     You know where. Just take me to that _____ great place with

1
Am

won - ders and wish - es.

2
Am
N.C.

won - ders and wish - es.

*Additional Lyrics*

Rap:    Angelica the one with all exposure,
         Dil is the one they drop in the stroller.
         And Tommy got the whole world on his shoulder,
         'Cause Dil cried to sleep till his eyes looked beat.
         And I couldn't have been Chucky, Chucky too petro.
         Chucky gets scared. Chucky said, "Let's go."
         If I was a Rugrat, it would have been so real.
         Me and my twin would have been just like Phil and Lil.

         And with one wish, blink, grant you one trip.
         Where we goin' this adventure? Who you wanna come with?
         See, you're my little brother that I'll come get, run wit.
         But it got to be done quick.
         Though Chucky is scared and Tommy is sad
         And Phil and Lil misses their mommy and dad.
         So pick a time and date and find a place,
         And I guarantee you that we all get home safe.

# TELL ME IT'S REAL

Words and Music by
RORY BENNETT
and JO JO HAILEY

Tell me it's real, ___ the feel-ing that ___ we feel. ___

___ Tell me that ___ it's real. ___ Don't ___ let love

come just ___ to pass us by. ___ Try is all we have ___ to do. ___

Tell Me It's Real - 6 - 1

*Verse 2:*
I can't explain the way you make me feel
Everytime that you told me that you loved me.
And you know you did, so many times.
Just when I thought that love could never be a part of me,
That's when you came along and showed me happiness.
Baby, you are the best.
I think you're different from the rest
And I really love you.
*(To Chorus:)*

# THANK U

Words by ALANIS MORISSETTE
Music by ALANIS MORISSETTE
and GLEN BALLARD

Thank U - 6 - 1

358

Thank U - 6 - 5

# THAT DON'T IMPRESS ME MUCH

Words and Music by
SHANIA TWAIN and R.J. LANGE

364

Verse 2:
I never knew a guy who carried a mirror in his pocket
And a comb up his sleeve, just in case.
And all that extra hold gel in your hair oughtta lock it,
'Cause heaven forbid it should fall outta place.
Oh, oh, you think you're special.
Oh, oh, you think you're something else.
(Spoken:) OK, so you're Brad Pitt.
(To Chorus:)

Verse 3:
You're one of those guys who likes to shine his machine.
You make me take off my shoes before you let me get in.
I can't believe you kiss your car good-night.
Come on, baby, tell me, you must be jokin', right?
Oh, oh, you think you're special.
Oh, oh, you think you're something else.
(Spoken:) OK, so you've got a car.
(To Chorus:)

# THEN THE MORNING COMES

Gtr. tuned down 1/2 step:
⑥ = E♭   ③ = G♭
⑤ = A♭   ② = B♭
④ = D♭   ① = E♭

Words and Music by
GREG CAMP

**Moderately** ♩ = 116

Guitar: ⟶ *C♯m*

Piano: ⟶ *Cm*

*Verse:*

1. Paint the town, take a bow, thank ev-'ry-bod-y.
2. Take your knocks, shake them off, duck ev-'ry-bod-y.

You're gon-na do it a-gain._____
You're gon-na take them a-gain._____

You are the few, the proud,__
You are your foe, your friend,__

Then the Morning Comes - 5 - 1

*To Coda*

N.C.

*Bridge:*

D.S. % al Coda

Coda

It's just the way that you walk.___

It's just the way that you talk,___ like it ain't no thing.___ And ev-'ry sin-gle

day is just a fling,___ then the morn-ing comes.

# UNINVITED

Words and Music by
ALANIS MORISSETTE

**Slowly**

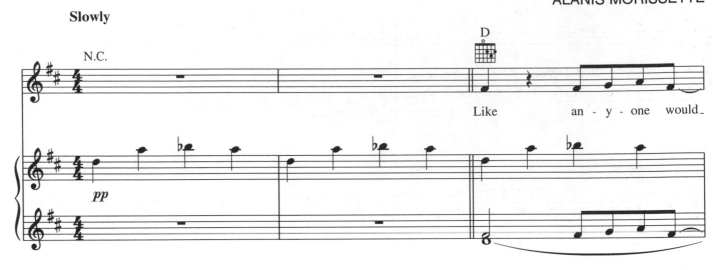

Like an-y-one would

be, I ___ am flat-tered ___ by your fas-ci-na-tion with ___ me.

Like an-y hot-blood-ed wo-man, I _____ have simp-ly _____

Uninvited - 5 - 1

Must be some-what heart-en - ing to ___ watch shep-herd ___
You ___ speak of my love ___ like you ___ have ex-per -

___ meet shep - herd. ___ But
- ienced love like mine be - fore. ___ But

you you're not al - lowed; ___ you're un-in-vit -
this is not ___ al - lowed; ___ you're un-in-vit -

- ed: an un-for-tu - nate slight.
- ed: an un-for-tu - nate slight.

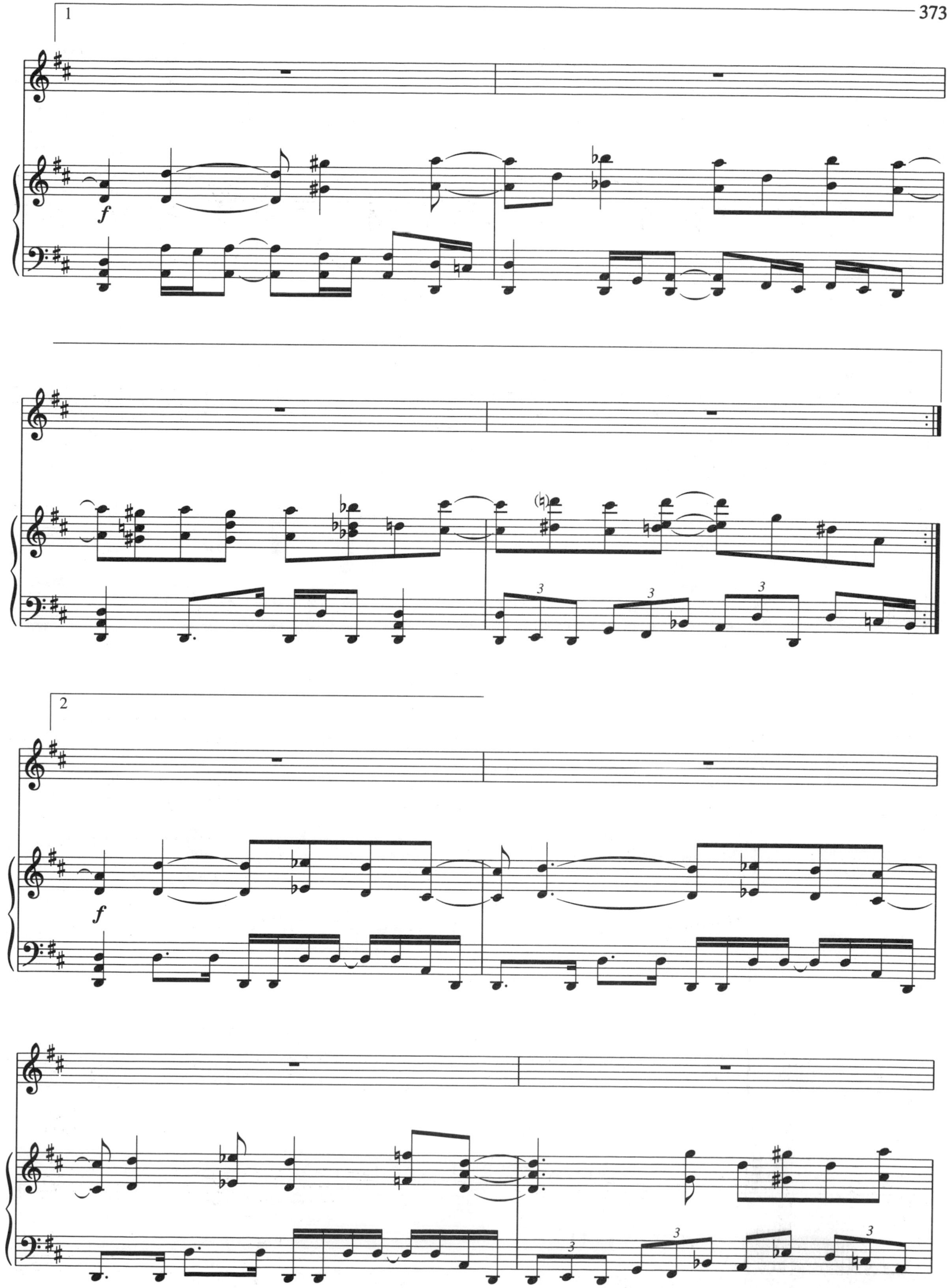
1
2
f
f

I don't think you un-wor - thy; I need a mo-

Gm          D

ment to de-lib-er - ate. _____          *Guitar solo ad lib.*

*pp*

*ff*

*8vb*

**Play 4 times**          D5

*8vb*

# WAIT

Lyrics by
ALAN and MARILYN BERGMAN

Music by
MICHEL LEGRAND

Wait - 5 - 1

be - fore you take your lips a - way from mine,_____ and where we are is where we've

been._____ Wait..._____

____ when you're in love the way we are, when ev - 'ry kiss and ev - 'ry

touch and ev - 'ry night is like a dream come true,_____

# WAITING FOR TONIGHT

Words and Music by MICHAEL GARVIN,
MARIA CHRISTENSEN and PHIL TEMPLE

Waiting for Tonight - 5 - 1

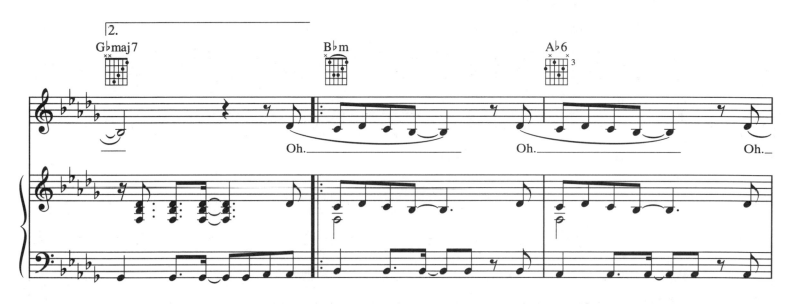

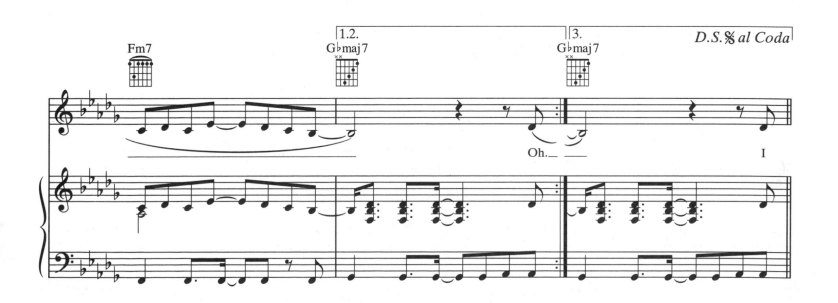

# WHERE MY GIRLS AT?

Words and Music by
MISSY ELLIOTT, ERIC SEATS
and RAPTURE

*Verse:*

1. See, he's my prop - er - ty, and an - y girl___ that
2. *See additional lyrics*

Where My Girls At? - 5 - 1

*Repeat ad lib. and fade*

girls at? From the front to back,__ well, is you feel-in' that? Put one hand up.__ Can you re-

peat that? Try-in' to take my man,__ see, I don't need__ that. Where my

*Verse 2:*
Hey, hey, hey, hey,
Don't you violate me
Cuz I'm-a make ya hate me.
If you decide to mess with mine,
Chop you down to size,
Make ya realize
You done messed up this time.
*(To Chorus:)*

# WILD WILD WEST
## (Main Theme)

Composed by
ELMER BERNSTEIN

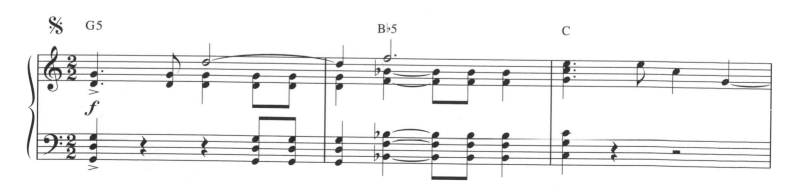

Wild Wild West - 5 - 1

# BIGGEST
## POP HITS & COUNTRY HITS
## OF 1998

## BIGGEST
## POP HITS OF 1998

(MF9820) Piano/Vocal/Chords
(AF9835) Easy Piano arr. Coates & Brimhall

- The biggest songs from the hottest artists
- More than 30 hit songs
- Available in P/V/C and Easy Piano Editions

*Titles (and artists) include:* **I Don't Want to Miss a Thing** (Aerosmith) • **My Heart Will Go On** (Celine Dion) • **How Do I Live** (LeAnn Rimes) • **You're Still the One** (Shania Twain) • **Ray of Light** (Madonna) • **All My Life** (K-Ci & Jo Jo) • **Good Riddance (Time of Your Life)** (Green Day) • **This Kiss** (Faith Hill) • **Kiss the Rain** (Billie Myers) • **Walkin' on the Sun** (Smash Mouth) and many more.

## BIGGEST
## COUNTRY HITS OF 1998

(MF9819) Piano/Vocal/Chords

- The top country songs of the year
- The hottest country artists
- All of your favorites collected together in one great folio

*Titles (and artists) include:* **You're Still the One** (Shania Twain) • **This Kiss** (Faith Hill) • **Nothin' But the Taillights** (Clint Black) • **There's Your Trouble** (Dixie Chicks) • **How Do I Live** (LeAnn Rimes) • **From This Moment On** (Shania Twain & Bryan White) • **I Do (Cherish You)** (Mark Wills) • **Cover You in Kisses** (John Michael Montgomery) • **Bad Day to Let You Go** (Bryan White) • **Holes in the Floor of Heaven** (Steve Wariner) and many more.

AD 0138

# 80 Years of Popular Music

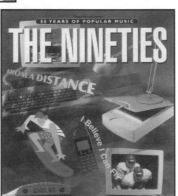

## The Sixties

Piano/Vocal/Chords
(MF9827)
ISBN 0-7692-6725-4  UPC 0-29156-95406-7
*Titles in this 82-song collection include:* **Aquarius/Let the Sun Shine In • Bad Moon Rising • California Girls • (Sittin' On) The Dock of the Bay • The House of the Rising Sun • I Got You Babe • I Saw Her Standing There • In-A-Gadda-Da-Vida • Itsy Bitsy Teeny Weenie Yellow Polka Dot Bikini • Mony, Mony • Oh, Pretty Woman • Raindrops Keep Fallin' on My Head • Soul Man • When a Man Loves a Woman • White Rabbit • Wipe Out** and more.

## The Seventies

Piano/Vocal/Chords
(MF9828)
ISBN 0-7692-6985-0  UPC 0-29156-95704-4
*Titles in this 58-song collection include:* **Baby I Love Your Way • Didn't I Blow Your Mind This Time • Go Your Own Way • A Horse with No Name • Hotel California • If You Don't Know Me By Now • I'll Take You There • Killing Me Softly with His Song • Love Train • My Sharona • Old Time Rock & Roll • The Rose • Stairway to Heaven • Time in a Bottle • What a Fool Believes • You Are So Beautiful** and more.

## The Eighties

Piano/Vocal/Chords
(MF9829)
ISBN 0-7692-6994-X UPC 0-29156-95742-6
*Titles in this 55-song collection include:* **Africa • Against All Odds (Take a Look at Me Now) • Arthur's Theme (Best That You Can Do) • Back in the High Life Again • Cuts Like a Knife • I Will Always Love You • In the Air Tonight • Like a Rock • Man in the Mirror • On the Wings of Love • (I've Had) The Time of My Life • Up Where We Belong • What's Love Got to Do with It • Words Get in the Way** and more.

## The Nineties

Piano/Vocal/Chords
(MF9830)
ISBN 0-7692-7103-0  UPC 0-29156-95950-5
*Titles in this 58-song collection include:* **All I Wanna Do • All My Life • Because You Loved Me • Foolish Games • I Believe I Can Fly • (Everything I Do) I Do It for You • I Don't Want to Miss a Thing • I Love You Always Forever • I Swear • I'll Be There for You (Theme from "Friends") • Kiss from a Rose • MMMBop • Quit Playing Games with My Heart • Sunny Came Home • Tears in Heaven • Un-Break My Heart • Walking on the Sun • You're Still the One** and more.